CRIES FROM THE

...ries and
... young boy
in India, to an African American teenager in the USA; from a sad and silent wife in Malaysia, to a terrified child in Uganda. But one thing is always the same. What makes them laugh or cry also makes us laugh or cry. Life is cruel if you are a child worker in a factory or a child soldier in a war; we feel their pain and fear too. The kindness of a street fruit-seller in Jamaica makes us happy; a loving wife making the last present for her sick husband makes us sad; and the story of the vet and Granny's cow in South Africa will surely make anyone smile . . .

BOOKWORMS WORLD STORIES

English has become an international language, and is used on every continent, in many varieties, for all kinds of purposes. *Bookworms World Stories* are the latest addition to the Oxford Bookworms Library. Their aim is to bring the best of the world's stories to the English language learner, and to celebrate the use of English for storytelling all around the world.

Jennifer Bassett
Series Editor

OXFORD BOOKWORMS LIBRARY
World Stories

Cries from the Heart

Stories from Around the World

Stage 2 (700 headwords)

Series Editor: Jennifer Bassett
Founder Editor: Tricia Hedge
Activities Editors: Jennifer Bassett and Christine Lindop

NOTE ON THE STORIES

The eight stories in this book were selected
from the twenty-six winning stories in the
2004 Commonwealth Short Story Competition.

Regional winner (Southern Africa):
Tod Collins (South Africa) for
'The Festive Season in a Part of Africa'

Winners of Highly Commended stories:
Sefi Atta (Nigeria) for 'The Photograph'
Jackee Budesta Batanda (Uganda) for 'Dora's Turn'
Janet Tay Hui Ching (Malaysia) for 'Callus'
Adrienne M Frater (New Zealand) for 'Leonard'
Lauri Kubuitsile (Botswana) for 'A Pot Full of Tears'
Anuradha Muralidharan (India) for 'Nimble Fingers'
Erica N Robinson (Jamaica) for 'The House'

RETOLD BY JENNIFER BASSETT

Cries from the Heart

Stories from Around the World

Illustrated by
Kwame Nyong'o

OXFORD UNIVERSITY PRESS

OXFORD
UNIVERSITY PRESS

Great Clarendon Street, Oxford OX2 6DP

Oxford University Press is a department of the University of Oxford.
It furthers the University's objective of excellence in research, scholarship,
and education by publishing worldwide in

Oxford New York

Auckland Cape Town Dar es Salaam Hong Kong Karachi
Kuala Lumpur Madrid Melbourne Mexico City Nairobi
New Delhi Shanghai Taipei Toronto

With offices in

Argentina Austria Brazil Chile Czech Republic France Greece
Guatemala Hungary Italy Japan Poland Portugal Singapore
South Korea Switzerland Thailand Turkey Ukraine Vietnam

OXFORD and OXFORD ENGLISH are registered trade marks of
Oxford University Press in the UK and in certain other countries

ACKNOWLEDGEMENTS

The stories are selected from the winning entries of the Commonwealth
Short Story Competition administered by the Commonwealth
Broadcasting Association and funded by the Commonwealth Foundation

The publishers are grateful to the following for permission to adapt and simplify copyright texts:
Sefi Atta for *The Photograph*; Jackee Budesta Batanda for *Dora's Turn*;
Janet Tay Hui Ching for *Callus*; Tod Collins for *The Festive Season in a Part of Africa*;
Adrienne M. Frater for *Leonard*; Lauri Kubuitsile for *A Pot Full of Tears*;
Anuradha Muralidharan for *Nimble Fingers*; Erica N. Robinson for *The House*

Word count (main text): 6,683 words

For more information on the Oxford Bookworms Library,
visit www.oup.com/elt/bookworms

CONTENTS

NOTE ON THE LANGUAGE

There are many varieties of English spoken in the world, and the characters in these stories sometimes use non-standard forms (for example, leaving out auxiliary verbs such as *am, are, is*). This is how the authors of the original stories represented the spoken language that their characters would actually use in real life.

There are also words that are usually only found in a particular variety of English (for example, *kraal* in South African English) and in some stories there are a few words from other languages (for example, *Afande* from Swahili). All these words are either explained in the stories or in the glossary on page 41.

NOTE ON THE ILLUSTRATOR

Kwame Nyong'o was born in Chicago, USA, and now lives in Nairobi in Kenya. He has been a freelance artist for many years, working in book illustration, animation, and character design. These are his first illustrations for a book for English language learners.

The Photograph

SEFI ATTA

⋈

A story from Nigeria, retold by Jennifer Bassett

In today's world there are photographs everywhere – web pages on the internet, magazines full of fashion and film stars, newspapers full of photos of war and sport, places and people from other lands.

They say a picture is worth a thousand words, and maybe it is, but what is the picture telling us? Sometimes we only see what we want to see . . .

*M*ake a picture in your mind: a girl with thin cheeks and tired eyes. Her arms and legs are as thin as sticks; she is only skin and bone. Clouds of dust circle above her head as the food trucks drive away. Their wheels leave marks on the dry ground, and soon only the marks show that the food trucks came to the village, and left.

The sun is at its hottest; the African sky is unending and cruel. Even the white men with cameras, busily taking photographs of the usual fighting over the food, are now getting ready to leave. They pack away their cameras, jump into their cars, and drive quickly away to cool, modern hotels in a city miles away. They are photojournalists.

One of them, sun-burned and hot, dressed in a shirt and jeans, kneels down on the dusty ground to take some photographs of the girl before he leaves. In the pocket of his shirt is a protein bar, soft from the sun, uneaten, untouched, forgotten.

He doesn't stop to think about the uneaten bar in his pocket and the starving girl. He is only one man. What can one man do in a world where life is cruel, and governments cannot or will not help their people? And who wants to stay in a place like this, with its dirt and its terrible smells, if they can drive away from it?

The girl caught the photographer's eye. She was in the middle of a group of boys, fighting just as strongly as they were, when the food trucks arrived. But she was pushed down and fell under the boys' feet. The boys stepped all over her, and when she could move again, the bags of rice were all gone. She stayed there, red-eyed, moving her fingers slowly over the dusty ground.

∞

The journalist takes his last photo, returns to America with his bag full of films. One of his photographs of the girl sells and is placed on the front cover of a news magazine.

'You've caught the face of hunger in Africa,' the news editor tells him.

*The girl stayed there, red-eyed, moving her fingers
slowly over the dusty ground.*

He wants to tell the editor that this photograph is just one face, in one village, in a country full of hungry faces. But he does not say it. The photograph is good for him. More people admire his work and want to buy his photographs for their magazines and newspapers.

The photograph is in most news stores by the end of the month, even in those bookstores where people go only to read the magazines and not to buy. They look at the face of the African girl, and quickly turn away to enjoy the rest of their shopping trip.

But the girl's picture stays in their minds.

A teenager has just finished looking at the clothes in *Vogue*, an expensive fashion magazine. She sees the photograph under the heading STARVING AFRICA. Her parents are from Africa. She herself was born and schooled in America, watching American TV, American films, and has never travelled out of America. She is uncomfortable with photographs like these. She remembers her classmates in school, who joke about starving Africans. She isn't African in *that* kind of way, but she isn't truly American either.

When she was younger, Cinderella, Snow White, and all the other girls and princesses in the Disney films didn't look like her. When she was older and became interested in fashion, the models on the magazine covers didn't look like her either. Then the magazines found out that Africa had beautiful women.

A Nigerian model is in the latest copy of *Vogue*, dressed in blue, and thin, so thin. The teenager feels the fat at the top of her legs. She wants to be thin like the model. She wants to wear jeans that are like a second skin. She wants a photograph of herself with cool, unsmiling eyes like the Nigerian model. She is careful about what she eats, and if she eats too much, she puts her finger down her throat to make herself sick.

Why does our world have people who starve, and people who decide to starve themselves? It doesn't matter why. The hunger inside this teenager is real. So she stares at the girl in the photograph, does not think about the dry dusty hungry land behind her, and admires her cheek bones.

⊃⊂

Leonard

ADRIENNE M FRATER

◉ ◉ ◉

A story from New Zealand, retold by Jennifer Bassett

*Women often knit gifts for their families.
Wives knit socks or scarves for their husbands;
grandmothers knit little jackets for their
children's babies.*

 *Buying a gift is quick and easy, but making
a gift with your own hands takes longer. And
if, like Leonard's wife, your hands are old
and stiff and crooked with arthritis, perhaps
knitting is not the best thing to do . . .*

'll knit him a scarf. Yes. I'll knit him a scarf the
same colour as his eyes.

I wait until my niece takes me shopping. 'I want to
buy some wool,' I tell her. 'I want to knit Leonard a
scarf.'

'But you don't knit,' she says. She looks at my crooked
hands and quickly looks away again. 'And Leonard
doesn't go out any more.'

But Petra takes me to the wool shop anyway.

'I want to buy some blue wool,' I say to the woman in
the shop. 'The colour of my husband's eyes.' I touch a
ball of blue wool that feels as soft as a bird's feathers.

'Isn't this a little too fine?' asks the woman in the shop.

'No, it's just right.'

◉ ◉ ◉

Later, tired after my shopping, I lie back in my armchair and have a little sleep.

When the car stops outside, I am still half asleep, and in my mind I see a younger Leonard standing at the door. His back is as straight as a piece of wood, and his blue eyes smile.

'Is anyone home?' Dan calls.

I wake with a jump.

'Here we are, Mr Phipps,' Dan says to Leonard. Holding Leonard's arm, Dan walks him into the house.

'Thank you, Dan.' I take off Leonard's coat and push some hair away from his eyes.

We eat dinner in a silence that aches. I drink red wine and Leonard eats with a spoon. Then, after I've washed him and put him to bed, I sit down to knit.

The needles are silver. The needles are cold. I take the paper cover off the wool, find one end of it, and try again and again to make the first stitch. I am listening to music by Beethoven, and it is nearly halfway through before I have finished the first row of stitches. My fingers hurt, and they won't do what I tell them. But I have begun.

◉ ◉ ◉

Leonard and I met at a concert in Auckland. He was tall, with blond hair then. I can still see him walking towards my seat. He took off the soft blue scarf that was the same colour as his eyes, and my heart gave a little jump. We talked over supper, and I found out where he lived and what he did.

'I'm an eye doctor,' he said, 'just beginning. No money, but I never miss concerts.'

I made our first date while we were walking out of the concert building. In those days men always did the asking, not girls. I don't know if Leonard was surprised at my asking him or not. He never said anything.

◎ ◎ ◎

On the days when Leonard goes to the day-care centre, I knit. I plan to finish the scarf for our fifty-third wedding anniversary. The scarf is almost finished, and when I hold it to the light, diamonds shine through. I shake the wool, drop a stitch, try to find it again. Was I more in love with Leonard than he was with me? I have so many questions . . . and I cannot ask any of them now.

'It's finished,' I tell my niece, putting the scarf round my neck.

'It looks good,' she said, 'if you don't look too closely. Is it a gift?'

'Yes. My last.'

On the morning of our anniversary I kiss Leonard and give him the scarf. I know he will not speak, but while I am putting the scarf round his neck, I find that I am still hoping.

*On the morning of our anniversary I kiss Leonard
and give him the scarf.*

The scarf is as crooked as my fingers. It's full of holes – long thin holes, little round holes. Leonard puts his hand up and touches the wool, and for one short moment, his eyes come alive again.

'Yes,' he wants to tell me. 'Yes,' he wants to say.

'The scarf is soft.

    The scarf is blue.

        The scarf is us.'

A Pot Full of Tears

LAURI KUBUITSILE

❏✦

A story from Botswana, retold by Jennifer Bassett

Luck comes and goes like a thief in the night, here one minute, gone the next. Some women want children but can't have them; others have children but can't keep them. Some babies are born into loving families; others never sleep in their own mother's arms, and never know their father's name.

And in the end, which of them is lucky, and which unlucky? Who can say?

The wind whispers through the walls of the little wooden house, blowing the flame of the smoky lamp from side to side. An old man sits, resting his arms on his legs, looking down at the wooden floor. How long will it be, he thinks. The end must come soon, it must.

Across the room from him sits a woman. She is a stranger and does not belong in this house. Everything about her is different – she looks different, she sounds different, she smells different. She has sat here in this poor little house for seven hours, but still the wind carries her expensive perfume, a smell from another world. She and the old man are different in every way, but she, too, sits on an old wooden chair, looking down at the wooden floor. How long will it be, she thinks. The end must come soon, it must.

Sometimes they hear a cry from the other room. Each time, the old man feels that cry all through his body, a father feeling a child's pain.

A loud scream brings both the old man and woman stranger to their feet. They wait. Minutes later, an old woman comes through the door, holding a baby in a blanket. The blanket is new, brought by the woman stranger. She now takes the baby from the old woman, but she does not move the blanket to look at the baby's face. She is not interested in that. She leaves the house without even a goodbye to the old man.

◻✶

It is months before. Before a baby is taken away in the night from a mother who is a child too young to be a mother. It is months before a father decides that he must lock his daughter in the back room. He must do this because he loves his daughter, and she will never find a good husband if people know her dark secret. It is months before a child with long feet like his father and a curved eyebrow like his mother is taken away in the night . . . A child who will never see the long feet of his father or the curved eyebrow of his mother.

It is morning, on that day months before, and a young

woman, hundreds of miles away, wakes up to find a little blood between her legs. Now her husband's family will decide that she can never have children. And her husband's mother will say, once again, that she is no good. She will say that a woman who cannot have children is no use to the family. Tears run down the young woman's face and she wants to die, because she does not want to give this news to her husband, who was hoping, hoping, hoping.

What can he do? He has fought with his mother again and again, but now he has to agree at last. He has to say, yes, he will take this barren woman back to her family. There is no use for her here. He is the only son of the house, and a wife who cannot have children is no use to him and his family.

The trouble is that he has learnt to like this woman who is his wife. Maybe he has even learnt to love her. He talks to her softly while she cries in his arms. We will do something, he tells her, we will do something.

They travel to a country which is at war, where the people live with death every day of their lives. And for these people, a baby who is taken away from them is a baby who has escaped from the house of death. This is what the woman tells them – the woman stranger who smells of expensive perfume. Now she is in the place where she belongs, in a cool modern office, with carpets on the floor and soft comfortable chairs. It will cost them money, the woman tells them – a small sum of money for

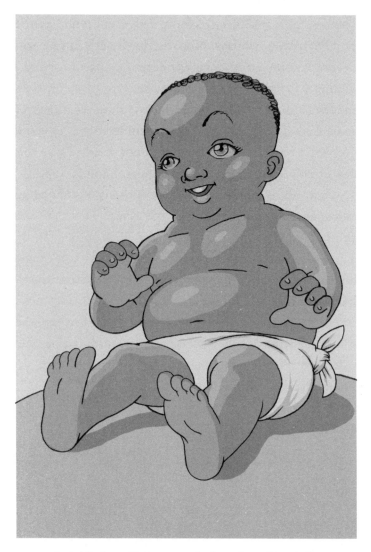

*A child who will never see the long feet of his father
or the curved eyebrow of his mother.*

this only son and his barren wife, but a very large sum of money for the old man in his wooden house. But he will not see that money. It is not for him.

Months later, the only son and his barren wife have a small boy; a baby with long feet and a curved eyebrow. They are happy. There is a grandson in the house, and the family name will continue. The boy will eat well every day, he will have the love of a family around him. He will never be hungry, he will never know war, he will never have to live in fear and in pain, without friends, without hope, without love.

◻✦

Years are gone, and a young married woman with a curved eyebrow cooks rice in a pot over an open flame. She looks at her small daughter, who shakes her fat little feet at the sky. And like a dream that never ends, the woman sees the long feet of a child who will never know where they came from. The tears run slowly down her cheek, falling, lost, in the steaming pot of rice.

○

The House

ERICA N ROBINSON

A story from Jamaica, retold by Jennifer Bassett

Sometimes people's lives go terribly wrong – maybe their marriage breaks down, they lose their job, their house, their friends; they have to live on the street, they drink too much, they don't wash . . .

Who will give a man like that a second chance? Only a very special kind of person – like Nan, a fruit-seller on the streets of Kingston . . .

Sonny had a new plan, but he did not know if Nan would agree to it.

He and Jake were building a house, which was big enough for two families. And one day they decided between them that Sonny's ex-wife Tanya and his children should have it.

'Nan,' Sonny said to her quietly, 'I going to let Tanya and the children live in the house.'

'What!' shouted Nan. 'Why?'

'It is good for the children,' said Sonny. 'They will be off the streets, and the boys won't have to hustle like me.'

'But what about me and you? Where we going to live?'

'We will try and build another one,' Sonny said.

Lord, he thought, is she going to leave me now? Maybe this is too much for her. I love her. I hope she understands what I'm trying to do.

'So . . .' Nan said slowly. 'You tell Tanya already?'

'I said something about it.' Sonny looked away from Nan's eyes. 'She agrees because it would be good for the children. I don't want my daughters living and dying like dogs on the streets of Kingston, and I don't want my boys carrying guns and selling drugs. I want them to have a place to live, Nan, a place where they can study their books and have a better life.'

'It is a hard thing you ask, Sonny,' Nan said quietly.

Sonny was a good man, and Nan trusted him. But she could not understand why he still cared about his ex-wife Tanya. Why can't he have a clean break with this woman, she thought. Tanya ruined his life – she went with other men and she kicked him out on the street. And then she sold all his things.

Nan remembered the day when she first met Sonny – a day that changed her life. He was just a street man, a drunkard, and so dirty. There was hunger in his face, in his eyes, even in the way he walked. She watched him for a while, then called out to him.

'Old man, come here. You hungry?'

'Yes, Ma'am.'

What kind of a street man was this, she thought. Nobody ever called her Ma'am. That wasn't a word people said to women who sold fruit on street corners. They usually called out 'old girl', or something worse like 'dutty sketel'. It felt good, to be called Ma'am.

She took some of her fruit and gave it to him.

'Thank you, Miss,' he said. 'I'm very grateful.'

He came by every day after that, and every day she gave him some fruit. Then one day she took him to the church on Harbour Street, which helped street people with their drink problems. They agreed to help him and took him in.

⌂ ⌂

Two months later a clean, tidy man in a light brown suit stopped by her stall and said, 'How are you, Madam?' He gave a big smile, showing his white teeth. 'Here's something for you,' he said, and held out two 1,000 dollar bills.

'Thank you,' Nan said, 'but why you giving me so much money?'

'You helped me when I needed someone,' he said quietly. 'You brought me back to life.'

Nan stared at him, not understanding.

'I was that old drunkard on the streets,' he explained, 'and you gave me food every day.'

'What!' said Nan. 'I happy to see that you alright now.'

*Sonny came by every day after that, and every day
Nan gave him some fruit.*

'Yes, thanks to you. I now have a job with the town council, you know. I drive the garbage truck.'

Nan smiled happily. She went on smiling for the next year and a half. She felt young again, and full of hope. At last she could forget the sad years when she was sixteen, with a baby, and no chance to go to school and get a better life for herself. She and Sonny started living together, and now they were planning to get married and have a home of their own. She decided to give Sonny this one thing, and to give it freely, because she trusted him.

'Okay, go on,' she said to Sonny, 'let them live in the house, and we will work together to build our own.'

Sonny put his long arms around Nan's comfortable body and pulled her close. He understood what she was saying – that she trusted him, that she was strong enough to wait.

He put his mouth close to her ear and whispered, 'Thank you.'

Dora's Turn

JACKEE BUDESTA BATANDA

✗

A story from Uganda, retold by Jennifer Bassett

War is always, in any place, at any time, a terrible thing. The heart cries out against the killing, but still it happens.

Somewhere in Uganda, Dora and her friend Acayo, who tells this story, are fighting in a war. They carry big AK-47 guns, and they know all about death and killing, pain and fear. They are children, twelve years old . . .

The little boy's cries are getting quieter, weaker. I can only just hear the words. 'Please, please . . . ah, no, no, no . . . Help me . . . help . . .'

Now there is a louder voice, the voice of Mad Tiger, our commander. He is fourteen years old.

'Hit him harder!' he shouts at us. 'Get closer to him. Use your whips – harder!'

The noise of our whips through the air is louder than the boy's cries.

'Our war is good,' shouts Mad Tiger. 'We must clean out bad people. We are soldiers – no escaping, no running away, everyone must fight.'

The other commanders smoke their cigarettes under a tree. 'Go on,' they laugh at us, 'get blood on your hands.'

The boy on the ground stops moving. Our whips are still. It is over.

✠

I feel ill. There is something hard in my throat, like a stone. I can't breathe. My friend Dora also tried to escape, and she'll be next. They will order me to kill her. Dora and I have been close. We are both twelve years old. Dora, who is going to be a doctor after the war . . . Dora, who wants to save lives, to stop the killing . . . Dora, who has been my friend when I wake in the night, screaming, because I can see the faces of all the people that I have killed . . .

The AK-47 is heavy on my shoulder, and I stand, waiting . . . waiting for Dora's turn, and the stone in my throat gets bigger.

'Acayo!' Mad Tiger shouts. I turn and look at him, hiding the fear in my eyes. It is a crime to show fear. My mouth is shut in a hard line. This helps to stop the tears coming into my eyes.

'Yes, *Afande*,' I say quietly. My voice must not be angry or unhappy or afraid, just quiet. That way he will not hear my fear. I give a soldier's salute to my commander, take my gun off my shoulder, and hold it up against my body. The gun points up to the black sky and the full moon. And the moon looks down at us, watching these deaths.

Mad Tiger smiles, his teeth shining white in the moonlight. He looks pleased. 'Are you ready?'

I cannot speak, but I nod my head.

They push Dora forward, and she falls on the ground in front of me, trembling. She is so small and thin, like a flower shaking in the wind. Our eyes meet. We cannot use words so we speak with our eyes. I don't want to do this, my eyes tell her.

But Mad Tiger and the other commanders are watching us, so I take Dora's arm and pull her to her feet. I want to ask her questions – Why did she try to escape without me? Why, Dora, why? We have always known each other's secrets before tonight.

Holding Dora's arm, I push her towards the trees. The killing will happen there, behind the trees, where no one can see. They are watching me, I can feel their eyes on my back. Perhaps they are following us, but I can't turn round to look. My legs are trembling. The stone in my throat gets bigger. My hands are hot and wet, and my fingers are making red marks on Dora's arm.

I take my hand away. I can't do this, not to Dora. We've been here together for three years.

'Don't be sorry,' Dora whispers. 'You have to do it. Everybody has to do it.'

She mustn't talk, someone will hear. Afraid, I look

Holding Dora's arm, I push her towards the trees. They are watching me, I can feel their eyes on my back.

behind me. We are alone. Quickly, I push Dora further into the trees. We stop.

I'm cold. I'm afraid.

'I can't do this,' I cry.

'You must,' Dora whispers. 'Or they'll kill you too.'

'Then they must kill us both.' The stone in my throat goes away with those words. 'You're my friend. We can run away . . . look for the government's soldiers . . . ask for help . . .' I speak excitedly. We can do it.

'Acayo,' Dora says, 'stop this talk. You know we—'

At that moment comes the sound of heavy guns behind us, where Mad Tiger and the others are.

'What . . .?' whispers Dora.

Suddenly I understand. Those are government army guns, not our guns. A helicopter gunship has found Mad Tiger's group.

'This is our chance!' I drop my gun and take hold of Dora's hand. 'Run!'

Dora stares at me, not sure.

'Do you still want to be a doctor?' I shout.

Suddenly Dora's feet come to life again. And the ground under our running feet trembles.

✄ ✄ ✄

Callus

JANET TAY HUI CHING

♡

A story from Malaysia, retold by Jennifer Bassett

Some people don't find it easy to talk about their feelings. If they have never talked about them, it can be hard to begin. And year after year, it gets harder and harder – just like a callus on the skin.

A wife watches while her husband packs his suitcase. A great change is coming into their lives, but maybe it is easier to talk about the suitcase . . .

She watched him pack his clothes and his wedding suit into his old suitcase. She could smell his cologne. When did he last wear cologne? Ah, at their wedding. It smelt strange then too. She never wore perfume. What use was perfume to a working woman like her? And married women who wear perfume are looking for lovers, trying to catch other men. That's what people say. She already had a good, hardworking husband with a shop of his own. What more can a woman want?

She began to feel better now, thinking about her good luck.

Lost in her thoughts, she jumped at the sound of the

suitcase shutting. His eyes went slowly round the room, looking for – what? She looked up at him.

'I put out all the clothes that you need,' she said. 'And you can't get any more in. It's a small suitcase.'

He looked at her for a moment. A Chinese girl like any other Chinese girl – small eyes, flat nose, smooth pale skin, and long straight hair, now pinned up tidily, in the way of married Chinese ladies. She wore her usual light blue samfoo. No, she was not a beauty, he thought, but she was a hard worker. His family was right when they said to him, 'She will make a very good wife, work hard for you, give you many sons.'

And it was true. He never had to complain about her, not once, from the day they married and moved into their new home, with his future in the same suitcase. Her face was the same now as it was then, neither soft nor hard, never showing what she felt or needed. He didn't know what she needed. And he never asked.

'It's a good suitcase. It's lasted a long time,' he said.

'Yes, I suppose. But it's still small.'

She got up from the bed and shook the pillows. They needed washing, she thought. Yes, wash it away, the dust and dirt of yesterday. Their past married life together. In the future nothing would ever be the same again.

'It's enough,' he said. 'I don't have so many things to put in it.' He put the suitcase on the floor, ready to go.

She looked at him, still smelling his cologne. Maybe it

Her face never showed what she felt or needed. He didn't know what she needed. And he never asked.

was the cologne that was making her feel afraid. She had to talk to him, tell him about her feelings. But she was a hard-working Chinese woman . . . and hard-working Chinese women must not have feelings.

'Is she waiting for you there?' she asked slowly.

'You mean the hotel?'

'Yes. I suppose the ceremony starts soon?'

She picked up one of the pillows and took off its cover. Yes, it needed washing. She wanted to get hold of him and shake him, scream and shout, and fall on her knees in front of him, crying 'No, no, please stay, don't go. I'll be a better wife. I'll work harder. I'll work as hard as two wives.' But she just stood there, saying nothing, doing nothing, her face showing nothing.

'I suppose,' he said.

'You'll be back in two days?'

He didn't want to talk about her feelings. She never did before. But then it wasn't every day that your husband brought home a new wife. A younger wife. Only nineteen. And beautiful because she was young and happy, and had big dark brown eyes – bright eyes. He only saw her once before he decided, but he remembered her eyes. It would be good to add her to the family, he thought. Now he would have two hard-working wives, one stronger than the other, but the young one would be like a new flower in the house. He picked up his suitcase.

'Yes, perhaps sooner. I don't know,' he said.

'I'll take care of the shop,' she said. 'When you come back . . . with her . . . I'll have some jobs for her to do.'

She sat on the bed again, suddenly feeling tired and old. He didn't understand. No one understood. She couldn't ask him not to go. People would say that she was wrong even to ask him.

'Of course,' he said. He was pleased that she thought of business. Business was important. He had many mouths to feed. He opened the door and turned to her.

'Today is a great day for our family. Not everyone is rich enough to have two wives. And there will be more sons to continue the family name.' He smiled at her.

'Yes. Not everyone . . . Husband?' She looked up at him, waiting, hoping.

'I have to go now. I'm late.' He did not want her to say anything. He never asked questions about her feelings because he was afraid of the answers. It was easier to pretend that she was happy all the time.

'Your suitcase. It's old. You need a new one.'

Thankfully, he turned away. No questions asked, no answers needed.

'Perhaps I will get a new one after all,' he said. He left the room and the door closed quietly behind him.

♡

Nimble Fingers

ANURADHA MURALIDHARAN

A story from India, retold by Jennifer Bassett

Life is never easy for the poor. They have to work long hours just to get a roof over their heads and one meal a day. If their children are lucky, they go to school. If they are not lucky, they have to work.

Krishna, who tells this story, is not lucky. He has to work in a factory making beedies, a kind of Indian cigarette. He is a good worker, because his young fingers are small and quick and nimble . . .

I cannot read or write, but I can count, but only up to 1500 because that is the number of beedies that I need to make in a day. My life is easy to explain. If I wake up early, I can play for about one hour, or until the sun begins to light up the eastern sky. For that one hour I am free – as free as the birds which sit on the tree outside my home.

My home is a hut with a roof of dried leaves. It is very small, but the three of us can just sleep in it. And I go away really early and come back in the nights, so only my mother and my little sister are there in the day time.

In the nights it is a bit crowded. When we sleep, my arm is often around little Thangachi, or Amma's thin foot is resting on my leg, but it doesn't matter.

The other day I asked Amma, 'How old am I?'

She counted on her fingers. 'Six.'

Six sounds very small when you think about 1500 beedies. But Saami, the owner of the factory where I work, always says that I have nimble fingers.

That night, when we were having our meal outside our home, I asked Amma,

'What does "nimble fingers" mean?'

'It means your fingers are like Weaver-Maama's fingers,' she said. 'When your uncle spins his cloth, have you seen how quickly his fingers move, pulling the threads this way and that way?'

I love to watch Weaver-Maama working, and now I am very happy because my fingers are like his.

I asked Amma one more question while we drank our rice soup.

'Why do I have to work with Saami and not with Weaver-Maama?'

This question made Amma unhappy, and when she is unhappy, she hits her head with her open hand. The noise is very loud, and she goes on hitting her head again and again, making a 'pat, pat, pat' sound.

It scares Thangachi and me, and I can see that the small one is ready to cry. I put my fingers – nimble fingers

'Why do I have to work with Saami and not with
Weaver-Maama?' I asked Amma.

– on Amma's hands to stop her hitting herself. She takes both my hands in her hand and starts crying into them. I can feel warm tears dropping onto my fingers.

Here I am, happy that I have Weaver-Maama's fingers, and Amma is crying. She looks at the black marks on my hands and the cuts on my finger ends – she kisses my hands, and holds me and Thangachi close to her.

'Amma,' I ask again, 'why can I not work with Weaver-Maama?'

Thangachi is pushing her finger into my back. Her eyes are telling me to stop my questions, but I want to know. If I can make 1500 beedies in a day, surely I can help Weaver-Maama weave his beautiful cloth?

✺

Amma never answered my question that day, but I just went on asking. I asked the same question every night until the next full moon.

That night Thangachi was already asleep. Amma and I were sitting outside watching fireflies dancing in the moonlight. Amma held me close to her and said:

'Krishna, you have to work all your life with Saami, the bonded labour man. You have to do this to pay back your grandfather's debt. You cannot work for another person because your grandfather has taken 5000 rupees and sold you to Saami. All your life you will have to work for him, in the same way as your father did.'

I look down to the ground, because I do not want

Amma to see the tears in my eyes. I am a brave boy, you see . . . but suddenly my nimble fingers don't feel so nimble any more.

The Festive Season in a Part of Africa

TOD COLLINS

◪

A story from South Africa, retold by Jennifer Bassett

If you are a poor farmer and you only have one cow, it is important that it doesn't get sick. Because if it does, and you need to get a vet to come and see it, that can be very expensive.

But if you are afraid that your cow will die, then you must send for the vet – even if it is the festive season and Christmas was only two days ago . . .

Two days after Christmas a Zulu woman and her schoolboy son sat waiting for me to finish my morning's clinic in Ondini. She wanted me to visit her old mother's cow, which had a calf waiting to be born. But for two days now the calf would not come out, and the poor cow was getting very tired. 'We have heard that you are a good vet,' the woman said to me.

So off we went. The schoolboy in the front of my pick-up, to show me the way, and the woman and my assistant Mbambo in the back. An hour of driving on bad roads full of holes and after that on dirt tracks. Then we stopped at an old empty kraal.

'Where's the cow?' I asked the boy.

'We walk a bit,' he said.

So we took my vet's black bags and we walked. Past other kraals with their fields and their fruit trees, and many of them with huts not lived in and falling down. We walked over rocks and by the side of rivers and after about forty-five minutes we came to a lonely kraal. There were three white huts, a clean tidy yard, and there under the fruit trees was the poor old cow, looking very, very tired.

They brought out two nice wooden chairs with colourful seats from the middle hut. I put my black bags on them, but first, I said hello in the proper Zulu way to Granny, who owned the cow. 'Inkosikazi' I called her. She was a very small woman, but she was the head of her family in the kraal.

Then I looked at the cow and found that the calf was still alive, and very, very big. So, with Mbambo helping me, I put the cow to sleep and did a caesarean.

When I finished, there was a crowd of about fifty people watching – men standing, older women sitting on the ground, children sitting in the fruit trees. Now the bullcalf was trying to stand on his feet, and shaking his head from side to side.

Someone brought a chair for Granny to sit on.

'We must talk about money. Is business now,'
Granny called out so everyone could hear.

'We must talk about money. Is business now,' she called out so everyone could hear.

'Well,' I said, 'you nearly had a dead cow and a dead calf, but I came and got the calf out, and so now they are both alive, not so?'

She agreed, and fifty other people agreed too.

'And I drove all the way from Ondini in my pick-up which is a thirsty car – as thirsty as an old man drinking beer on a Sunday.'

Smiles and laughter.

'And if you take good care of this calf and he grows into a strong young bull, when he is a year old, at the market in Ondini, they will pay you 1,500 rands for him. Not so?'

'Yes.' The old men in the crowd nodded their heads.

'And the cow . . . she is old and tired, and the flies are very bad this summer. But if she lives, next autumn you can sell her for over 2,500 rands.'

Loud noises of agreement from the crowd.

'So then, Inkosikazi, my work has given you about 4,000 rands that you didn't have before.'

'Yes.'

'So how about we go halves – and I take 2,000 rands?'

Much whispering between Granny and her friends.

'That's lots of money,' she said.

'Yes, it is,' I said, 'and we have just had Christmas and soon it will be New Year, and maybe the cow will die. So it is better that I don't ask for so much. You can pay me just half of that – 750 rands.'

Louder whispering and nods of agreement.

'But!' said the schoolboy, who was standing behind his grandmother, 'half of 2,000 is not 750, it is 1,000!'

'Oh-ho!' I said. 'I can see you are a clever young man. I made a mistake, but if I said 750, then I shall still say 750 and not change it.'

Well, what a noise there was after that! Everybody was smiling and happy. Granny pulled out a great big handful of 200 rand notes, and she gave four of them to me, with her other hand open upwards next to the giving hand, in the proper Zulu way.

I took the money from her with my two open hands side by side, in the proper Zulu way, counted the notes and said, 'Inkosikazi, you have given me too much.'

She stood up and said, 'Keep the 50, it is for your assistant Mbambo.'

Man, the season of goodwill is amazing.

Then we walked back for an hour, mostly uphill, with a long line of helpers carrying my bags. We stopped sometimes to eat the sweet wild fruit that grows around most of the old kraals in this part of Africa . . .

. . . in the festive season.

GLOSSARY

admire to think that something or somebody is very good

Afande (*Swahili*) a title of respect, like *Sir* in English

amazing very surprising

anniversary a day exactly one year (or more) after a special event

arthritis a disease which causes pain in the joints of the body

assistant a person who helps another person in their work

barren (in this story) not able to have children

bonded labour a kind of slavery, when somebody has to work for nothing, usually in bad conditions, to pay off a debt

breathe to take in and let out air through the nose and mouth

caesarean cutting the mother's body to take out a baby

calf (bull calf) a baby cow (a male calf)

callus a place of hard thick skin on a hand or foot

ceremony a formal public event (e.g. a wedding)

cheek the soft part of the face below the eyes

cloth material made of wool, cotton, etc.

cologne a kind of light perfume

complain to say you don't like or are unhappy about something

concert a public performance of music

council a group of people who make rules for a town, city, etc.

crooked not straight

cruel very unkind

curved having a round shape

date a meeting with a boy/girlfriend or a possible boy/girlfriend

debt money that you must pay back to somebody

diamond a very expensive, hard stone that looks like clear glass

drug a dangerous thing that people put in their bodies because it makes them feel happy, excited, different, brave, etc.

drunkard somebody who gets drunk very often

dutty (*West Indian English*)   dirty
editor   a person who prepares a newspaper before it is printed
ex-wife   a person's former wife
eyebrow   the line of hair above the eye
feelings   something (e.g. anger, fear) that you feel inside yourself
festive   connected with the days when people celebrate Christmas
flame   the red/orange part of a fire
garbage (*North American English*)   rubbish
goodwill   friendly or helpful feelings towards other people
government   the people who make laws and control the country
hustle (*North American English*)   to sell things (e.g. drugs, guns)
    outside the law
hut   a small simple building with one room
Inkosikazi (*Zulu*)   a word for Mrs, wife, madam
joke   something that you do or say to make people laugh
knit   to make clothes from wool using two long sticks (needles)
kraal (*South African English*)   a village of huts with a place for
    keeping animals
lamp   a thing that gives light
mind (*n*)   the part of you that thinks and remembers
model   a person who wears clothes for photographs
niece   the daughter of your brother or sister
nimble   able to move quickly and easily
pale   with not much colour
perfume   a liquid with a nice smell that you put on your body
pillow   a soft thing you put your head on when you are in bed
protein bar   like a bar of chocolate, but made of fruit, nuts, etc.
ruin (*v*)   to do great harm or damage to something
rupee   the unit of money in India and Pakistan
salute (*n*)   the sign that soldiers make, lifting the hand to the
    head
samfoo (*Cantonese*)   jacket and trousers, worn by Chinese women

scare (*v*) to make somebody frightened

scarf a piece of material that you wear around your neck or head

sketel (*West Indian English*) a woman who has too many men friends

spin (*v*) to make thread from wool or cotton

starving in danger of dying because you do not have food to eat

stitch (*n*) a circle of wool round a needle when you are knitting

thread a long thin piece of wool, cotton, etc.

throat the part inside your neck where food and air go down

track a rough path or road

tremble to shake because you are cold, afraid, or ill

truck a big vehicle for carrying heavy things

trust (*v*) to believe that someone is good and will not hurt you

vet a doctor for animals

war fighting between countries, or between groups of people

weave to make cloth by putting threads over and under one another

whip (*n*) a long piece of rope with a handle, for hitting animals

Zulu a member of a race of black people in South Africa

ACTIVITIES

Before Reading

Before you read the stories, read the introductions at the beginning. Then use these activities to help you think about the stories. How much can you guess about them?

1 *The Photograph* (story introduction page 1). Do you agree (A) or disagree (D) with these ideas?

1 Photographs give stronger messages than words.
2 Photographs can lie.
3 People understand photographs more easily than words.

2 *Leonard* (story introduction page 6). What can you guess? Choose two endings.

Leonard's wife will knit a scarf for Leonard . . .
1 which will be beautiful.   3 because she loves him.
2 which will be full of holes.   4 because he is cold.

3 *A Pot Full of Tears* (story introduction page 11). What do you think? Choose (a) or (b).

It is better for children to have . . .
a) a hungry, difficult life, but to stay with their own mother.
b) an easy, comfortable life with a woman who is not their real mother.

4 *The House* (story introduction page 16). **What can you guess about Nan? Choose from these ideas. She . . .**

is cruel	cries a lot	helps people	doesn't help people
is kind	smiles a lot	trusts people	doesn't trust people

5 *Dora's Turn* (story introduction page 21). **What can you guess about this story? Choose yes (Y) or no (N).**

1 This story will be about soldiers and war and killing. Y/N
2 This story will have a happy ending. Y/N

6 *Callus* (story introduction page 26). **Do you agree (A) or disagree (D) with these ideas?**

1 It is always better for people to talk about their feelings.
2 Sometimes it is better to keep silent about your feelings.
3 Women are good at talking about feelings; men are not.

7 *Nimble Fingers* (story introduction page 31). **What can you guess about Krishna? Choose true (T) or not true (NT).**

1 He does not go to school now. T / NT
2 One day he will go to school. T / NT

8 *The Festive Season in a Part of Africa* (story introduction page 36). **How many of these things will happen?**

1 The cow dies.
2 The cow has a calf.
3 The vet is very expensive.
4 The vet agrees a good price.

ACTIVITIES

After Reading

1 Match these parts of sentences about people in these eight stories. There are three parts to each sentence. Then choose the best linking words to join the parts together.

First parts of the sentence:

1 The African girl in the photograph is starving, . . .
2 Mrs Phipps is knitting a scarf for Leonard, . . .
3 A woman and her husband cannot have children, . . .
4 Sonny was a drunkard living on the streets, . . .
5 Dora and Acayo are soldiers with guns, . . .
6 A man packs his suitcase to go to his wedding . . .
7 Krishna works in Saami's factory making beedies . . .
8 Granny in South Africa sends for the vet . . .

Second parts of the sentence:

9 *because / so* they buy a baby in another country . . .
10 *while / after* his first wife watches him unhappily . . .
11 *so / because* she is afraid her cow will die, . . .
12 *but / so* the girl in the bookstore in the USA admires her cheek bones . . .
13 *who / what* are fighting in a terrible war, . . .
14 *and / after* he asks his mother every night for a month . . .
15 *which / who* has been her husband for fifty-three years, . . .
16 *but / because* Nan gave him some fruit . . .

Third parts of the sentence:

17 *because / but* they are only children, twelve years old.

18 *and / after* does not think about dying from hunger.

19 *why / because* he cannot work with his uncle, Weaver-Maama.

20 *but / because* he spoke nicely to her and called her Ma'am.

21 *but / so* now he does not remember her name.

22 *because / but* the calf is born alive and all is well.

23 *so / and* tries to find the words to stop him going.

24 *who / and* take the baby back to their home as their son.

2 **How did you feel about the people in these stories? Use the list of names and the table below to make sentences about them. Use as many words as you like to finish the sentences.**

1 *The Photograph*: the photographer / the American girl

2 *Leonard*: Leonard / Leonard's wife

3 *A Pot Full of Tears*: the girl who had a baby / the woman who could not have a baby / the baby with long feet

4 *The House*: Sonny / Nan

5 *Dora's Turn*: Dora / Acayo / Mad Tiger

6 *Callus*: the wife / the husband

7 *Nimble Fingers*: Krishna / Krishna's mother

I felt	afraid for angry with pleased with sorry for	....	when because	....

3 Use the clues to complete the crossword with words from the stories (one word from each story). All words go across.

1 Nan in Jamaica agreed about the house because she _____ Sonny.

2 Acayo's legs _____ because she is so afraid.

3 The cow in South Africa had a _____ waiting to be born.

4 The African baby with long feet had a _____ eyebrow.

5 Krishna in India wanted to help his uncle to _____ cloth.

6 Leonard's wife _____ him a scarf which was full of holes.

7 The Chinese wife wanted to talk about her _____ but her husband did not want to hear.

8 The _____ inside the American teenager is not for food.

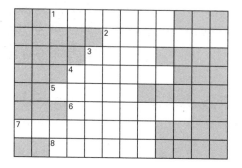

4 There are two hidden words (of 8 letters and 3 letters) in the completed crossword above. What are they? Which stories do they come from? What do they mean?

Word 1 _____

Word 2 _____

5 In *The Festive Season in a Part of Africa*, why did the vet say that half of 2,000 rands was 750, not 1,000? Look at these two ideas, and decide which one is best for the story.

1 He made a mistake because he was not good at numbers.

2 He did not really make a mistake; he wanted to give Granny a good price because it was the festive season.

6 Here is a short poem (a kind of poem called a haiku) about one of the stories. Which of the eight stories is it about?

> African baby,
> taken away in the night,
> bought and sold like gold.

Here is another haiku, about the same story.

> Does a baby cry
> for a mother and father
> he has never seen?

A haiku is a Japanese poem, which is always in three lines, and the three lines always have 5, 7, and 5 syllables each, like this:

| Does | a | ba | by| cry | = 5 syllables
| for | a | mo | ther | and | fa | ther | = 7 syllables
| he | has | nev | er | seen? | = 5 syllables

Now write your own haiku, one for each of the other seven stories. Think about what each story is really about. What are the important ideas for you? Remember to keep to three lines of 5, 7, 5 syllables each.

ABOUT THE AUTHORS

SEFI ATTA

Sefi Atta (1964–) was born in Lagos, Nigeria. She was educated in Nigeria, England, and the United States, and worked for many years as a qualified accountant. She lives in Mississippi, USA, with her husband and daughter, and teaches at a university. Her short stories have won several awards, and she has written plays for the radio and the theatre. Her first novel, *Everything Good Will Come*, was published in 2005, and in 2006 it won the first Wole Soyinka Prize for Literature in Africa.

ADRIENNE M FRATER

Adrienne Frater lives and writes in Nelson, New Zealand. She was a teacher for many years, but is now a full-time writer, writing stories for both adults and children. She loves to travel, and writes anywhere – on boats or in a motorhome. The idea for her story *Leonard* came to her like this. Her friend's son made a beautiful wooden box for his mother, out of old wood, but the wood was thin and had holes in it. It was a present full of holes, but made with great love, like the scarf in the story.

LAURI KUBUITSILE

Lauri Kubuitsile was born in the USA and came to Botswana in 1989 as a United States Peace Corps Volunteer. After some years as a science teacher in schools in Mahalapye, she became a writer and author. Her short stories have appeared in magazines around the world, and have won several prizes. She also writes for newspapers, and her first book, *The Fatal Payout*, was published in 2005. She is married, and lives in Botswana with her husband and two teenaged children.

ERICA N ROBINSON

Erica Robinson-Sturridge was born in the town of Mandeville in Jamaica, where she spent her early years. As a child, she loved reading and writing, and playing on the beach, and she continued to read literature while she was studying at university for her degrees in biology and nutrition. She still works as a scientist, but hopes one day to be a full-time writer. She lives with her husband in her hometown in Jamaica.

JACKEE BUDESTA BATANDA

Jackee Budesta Batanda was born in Uganda, and lives in Kampala. She read a lot as a child, and at the age of fourteen decided to be a writer because she wanted 'to create stories that captivate and enchant readers around the world'. Many of her short stories have won prizes, and she has published a children's book, *The Blue Marble*. She has also written a collection of short stories, *Everyday People*, and is currently at work on a novel.

JANET TAY HUI CHING

Janet Tay Hui Ching (1976–) was born in Malaysia, and was educated in Sarawak and at university in England. She worked as an advocate and solicitor for five years in Kuala Lumpur, Malaysia, before leaving the legal profession to become an editor at a local publishing house. The idea for her story *Callus* came to her while listening to stories told at a family party for her grandmother's birthday.

ANURADHA MURALIDHARAN

Anuradha Muralidharan lives in Bangalore, India, with her husband and son, and works as a manager in marketing communications. She has a Master's in English Literature, and has wanted to be a writer since she was a small child. Her first book, *The Coconut Cutter and Other Stories*, came out in 2000, and a novel, *Wingless*, was published in 2004. She is very interested in social questions, and the idea for her story *Nimble Fingers* came to her while reading about bonded labour on the internet.

TOD COLLINS

Tod Collins is a South African whose family came to Natal in the mid-1850s. As a child he lived on a farm, and later studied veterinary science, becoming a qualified vet in 1973. He now lives in a small mountain village, where he works as a vet and climbs mountains in his spare time. He is not a professional writer, he says. He writes mostly to keep a record for his family, but he enjoys describing his adventures as a country vet and his experiences in the mountains of KwaZulu-Natal and Lesotho.

OXFORD BOOKWORMS LIBRARY

Classics • Crime & Mystery • Factfiles • Fantasy & Horror
Human Interest • Playscripts • Thriller & Adventure
True Stories • World Stories

The OXFORD BOOKWORMS LIBRARY provides enjoyable reading in English, with a wide range of classic and modern fiction, non-fiction, and plays. It includes original and adapted texts in seven carefully graded language stages, which take learners from beginner to advanced level. An overview is given on the next pages.

All Stage 1 titles are available as audio recordings, as well as over eighty other titles from Starter to Stage 6. All Starters and many titles at Stages 1 to 4 are specially recommended for younger learners. Every Bookworm is illustrated, and Starters and Factfiles have full-colour illustrations.

The OXFORD BOOKWORMS LIBRARY also offers extensive support. Each book contains an introduction to the story, notes about the author, a glossary, and activities. Additional resources include tests and worksheets, and answers for these and for the activities in the books. There is advice on running a class library, using audio recordings, and the many ways of using Oxford Bookworms in reading programmes. Resource materials are available on the website <www.oup.com/elt/bookworms>.

The *Oxford Bookworms Collection* is a series for advanced learners. It consists of volumes of short stories by well-known authors, both classic and modern. Texts are not abridged or adapted in any way, but carefully selected to be accessible to the advanced student.

You can find details and a full list of titles in the *Oxford Bookworms Library Catalogue* and *Oxford English Language Teaching Catalogues*, and on the website <www.oup.com/elt/bookworms>.

THE OXFORD BOOKWORMS LIBRARY
GRADING AND SAMPLE EXTRACTS

STARTER • 250 HEADWORDS

present simple – present continuous – imperative –
can/cannot, must – going to (future) – simple gerunds ...

Her phone is ringing – but where is it?

Sally gets out of bed and looks in her bag. No phone. She looks under the bed. No phone. Then she looks behind the door. There is her phone. Sally picks up her phone and answers it. ***Sally's Phone***

STAGE 1 • 400 HEADWORDS

... past simple – coordination with *and, but, or* –
subordination with *before, after, when, because, so* ...

I knew him in Persia. He was a famous builder and I worked with him there. For a time I was his friend, but not for long. When he came to Paris, I came after him – I wanted to watch him. He was a very clever, very dangerous man. ***The Phantom of the Opera***

STAGE 2 • 700 HEADWORDS

... present perfect – *will* (future) – *(don't) have to, must not, could* –
comparison of adjectives – simple *if* clauses – past continuous –
tag questions – *ask/tell* + infinitive ...

While I was writing these words in my diary, I decided what to do. I must try to escape. I shall try to get down the wall outside. The window is high above the ground, but I have to try. I shall take some of the gold with me – if I escape, perhaps it will be helpful later. ***Dracula***

STAGE 3 • 1000 HEADWORDS

... should, may – present perfect continuous – *used to* – past perfect – causative – relative clauses – indirect statements ...

Of course, it was most important that no one should see Colin, Mary, or Dickon entering the secret garden. So Colin gave orders to the gardeners that they must all keep away from that part of the garden in future. *The Secret Garden*

STAGE 4 • 1400 HEADWORDS

... past perfect continuous – passive (simple forms) – *would* conditional clauses – indirect questions – relatives with *where/when* – gerunds after prepositions/phrases ...

I was glad. Now Hyde could not show his face to the world again. If he did, every honest man in London would be proud to report him to the police. *Dr Jekyll and Mr Hyde*

STAGE 5 • 1800 HEADWORDS

... future continuous – future perfect – passive (modals, continuous forms) – *would have* conditional clauses – modals + perfect infinitive ...

If he had spoken Estella's name, I would have hit him. I was so angry with him, and so depressed about my future, that I could not eat the breakfast. Instead I went straight to the old house. *Great Expectations*

STAGE 6 • 2500 HEADWORDS

... passive (infinitives, gerunds) – advanced modal meanings – clauses of concession, condition

When I stepped up to the piano, I was confident. It was as if I knew that the prodigy side of me really did exist. And when I started to play, I was so caught up in how lovely I looked that I didn't worry how I would sound. *The Joy Luck Club*

MORE WORLD STORIES FROM BOOKWORMS